Be An Expert!™

Baby Animals

Rebecca Silverstein

Children's Press®
An imprint of Scholastic Inc.

Contents

Know the Babies

Be an expert! Get to know the names of these baby animals!

Baby Lions

They are called cubs.
They grow up in a group
called a pride.

Animal Answers

Q: How do lion cubs get clean?

A: A mother lion cleans her cubs by licking them.

Baby Sheep

They are called lambs.
They are covered in soft **fleece**.

Expert Fact

Lambs stand up and walk soon after they are born.

Baby Kangaroos

They are called joeys. The mother kangaroo carries the joey in her **pouch**.

Zoom In

Find these parts in the big picture.

| pouch | tail | ears | paws |

Baby Penguins

They are called chicks. They are covered in soft feathers called down.

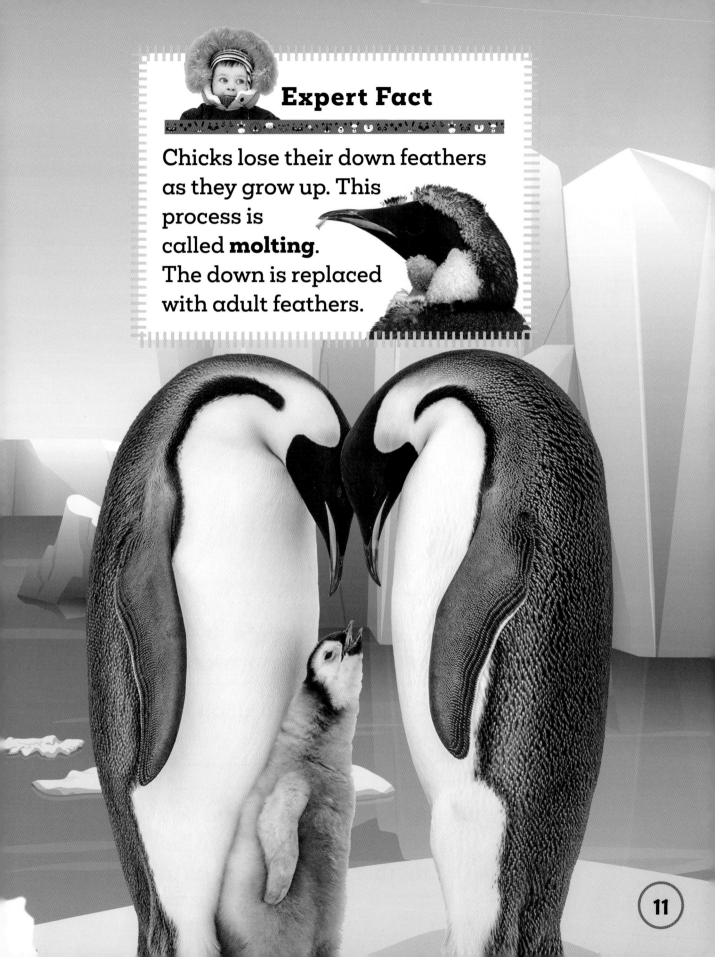

Expert Fact

Chicks lose their down feathers as they grow up. This process is called **molting**. The down is replaced with adult feathers.

Baby Elephants

They are called calves.
They are huge!

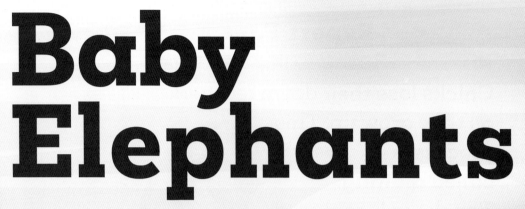

Animal Answers

Q: How big is an elephant when it is born?

A: A newborn calf can be as tall as a three-year-old kid! Its mother is three times as tall.

Baby Ducks

They are called ducklings.
They follow their mother
everywhere!

Zoom In

Find these parts in the big picture.

bill   **tail**   **webbed foot**   **eye**

15

Baby Rabbits

They are called kits.
They cannot hop right away.
They crawl instead.

Animal Answers

Q: Does a mother rabbit have one kit at a time?

A: No. She has many kits at once. That group is called a **litter**.

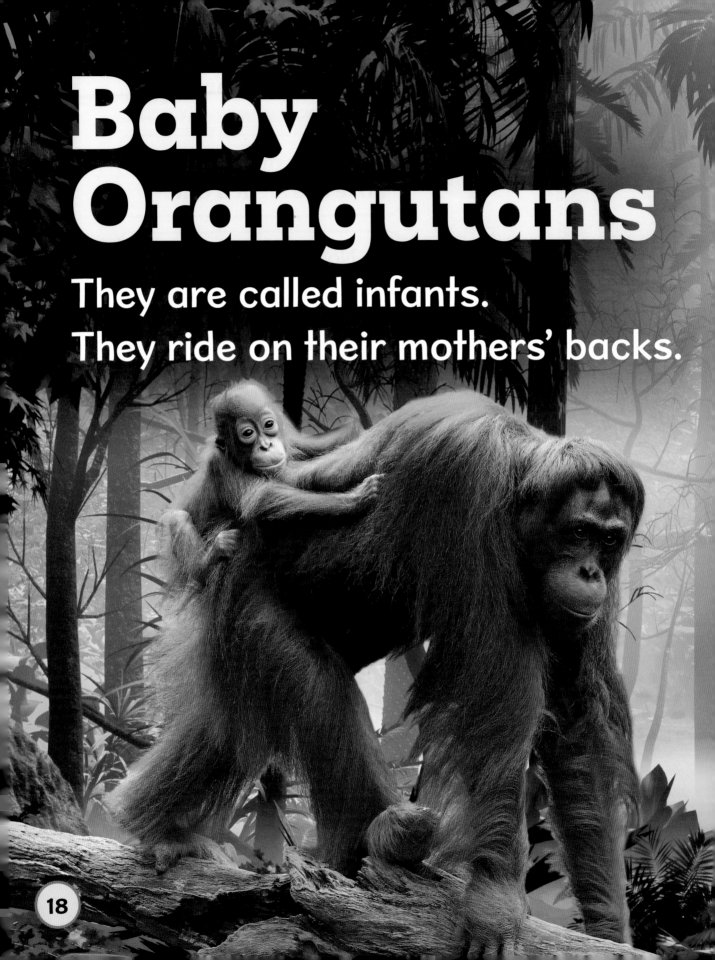

Baby Orangutans

They are called infants.
They ride on their mothers' backs.

Expert Fact

Baby orangutans are not the only animals called infants. Baby humans are called infants too!

All the Baby Animals

They are so cute.

Hooray for baby animals!

1.

2.

5.

6.

Expert Quiz

Can you name each of these baby animals? Then you are an expert! See if someone else can name them too!

3.

4.

7.

8.

Answers: 1. Lamb, 2. Duckling, 3. Kits, 4. Infant, 5. Joey, 6. Calf, 7. Chicks, 8. Cubs.

21

Expert Gear

Meet a veterinarian. What does she need to take care of baby animals?

She needs **scrubs**.

She needs **gloves**.

She needs an **otoscope**.

She needs a **stethoscope**.

Glossary

fleece (FLEES): the woolly coat of a sheep.

litter (LIT-ur): a number of baby animals that are born at the same time to the same mother.

molting (MOHL-ting): losing old fur, feathers, shell, or skin so that new ones can grow.

pouch (POWCH): a pocket in the kangaroo mother's body in which she carries her young.

Index

Library of Congress Cataloging-in-Publication Data

Names: Silverstein, Rebecca, author.

Title: Baby animals/Rebecca Silverstein.

Other titles: Be an expert! (Scholastic Inc.)

Description: Book edition. | New York: Children's Press, an imprint of Scholastic Inc., 2022. | Series: Be an expert; 15 | Includes index. | Audience: Ages 3–5. | Audience: Grades K–1. | Summary: "Baby lions are called cubs. Baby penguins are called chicks. They are so cute! What do you know about baby animals? With this book, you can become an expert! Feel like a pro with exciting photos, expert facts, and fun challenges. Do you know what baby sheep are called? What about baby ducks? Try it! Then see if you can pass the Expert Quiz!"—Provided by publisher.

Identifiers: LCCN 2021025675 (print) | LCCN 2021025676 (ebook) | ISBN 9781338797848 (library binding) | ISBN 9781338797855 (paperback) | ISBN 9781338797862 (ebk)

Subjects: LCSH: Animals—Infancy—Juvenile literature. | BISAC: JUVENILE NONFICTION / Animals/Baby Animals | JUVENILE NONFICTION/ Science & Nature/General (see also headings under Animals or Technology).

Classification: LCC QL763.S5185 2022 (print) | LCC QL763 (ebook) | DDC 591.3/92—dc23

LC record available at https://lccn.loc.gov/2021025675

LC ebook record available at https://lccn.loc.gov/2021025676

10 9 8 7 6 5 4 3 2 1   22 23 24 25 26

Printed in Heshan, China 62

First edition, 2022

Series produced by Spooky Cheetah Press

Design by The Design Lab, Kathleen Petelinsek

Cover design by Three Dogs Design LLC

Photos © cover: Chris Hepburn/Getty Images; 1 top left: Martin Ruegner/Getty Images; 11 inset bottom: Nature Picture Library/Alamy Images; 16–17 foreground: blickwinkel/Alamy Images; 17 inset top: Lane Oatey/Blue Jean Images/Getty Images; 23 center bottom: Nature Picture Library/Alamy Images.

All other photos © Shutterstock.